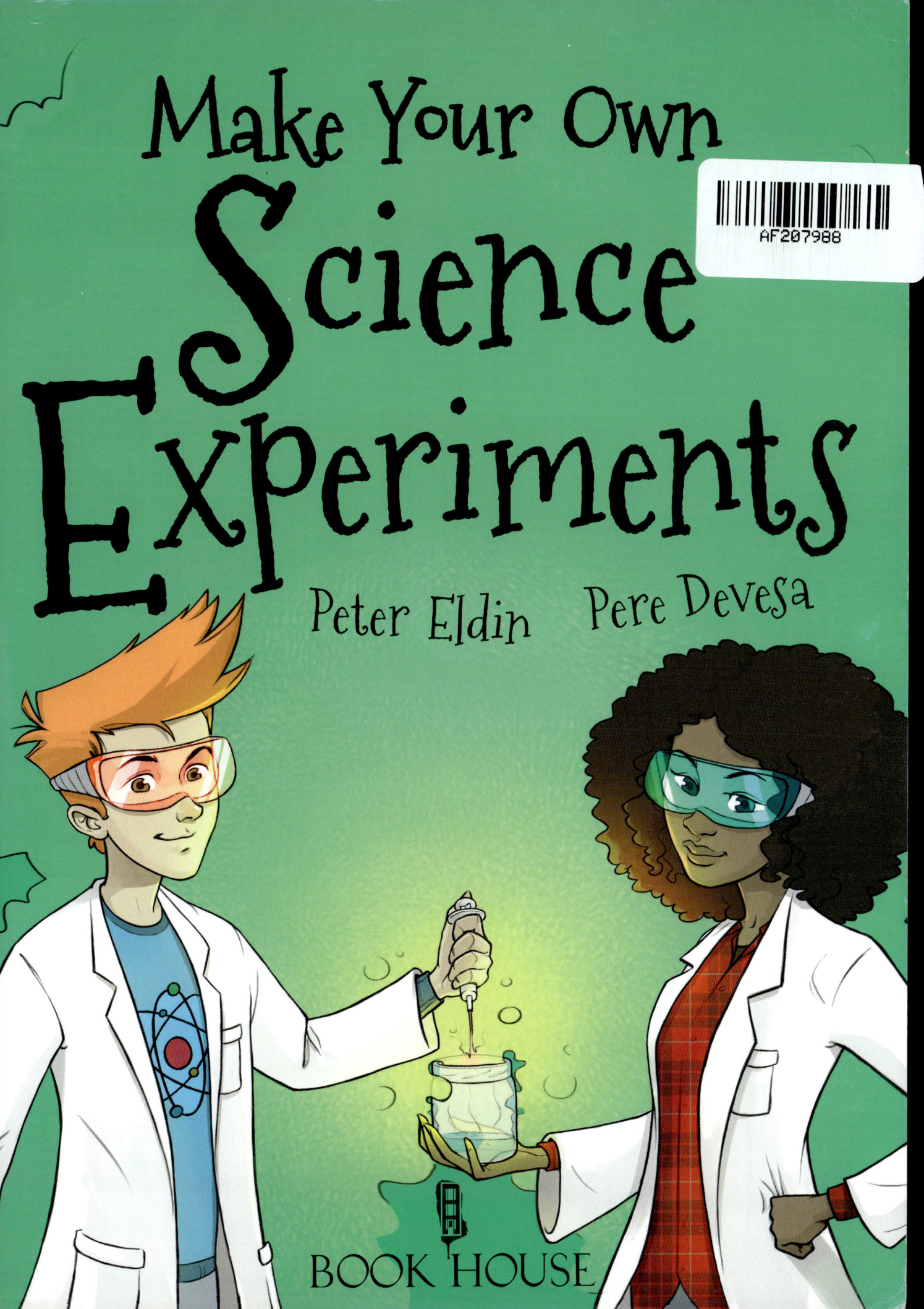

Make Your Own Science Experiments

Peter Eldin Pere Devesa

BOOK HOUSE

Science is fun

Science isn't just formulas and theories — it can be lots of fun too!

All of the experiments in this book are designed to be enjoyable. At the same time, you will learn a little about the science of the world around you. If you want to show these experiments to your friends or family, try them out a few times in private first.

Materials

You don't need any special equipment to try the science experiments in this book.

All the projects can be done with items you will have at home or that are easily obtainable. These include: thin card, paper, pens, scissors, toothpicks, coins, salt, soap, wood, washing-up liquid, round cheese boxes, spoons, string, paper clips, combs, modelling clay, and even an egg and a potato!

That rings a bell

Sound travels by vibrations in the air. But air is not a very good conductor of sound. String, which carries the vibrations, is a better conductor so you hear the sound more clearly.

You will need:
- Spoon
- String
- Two ears

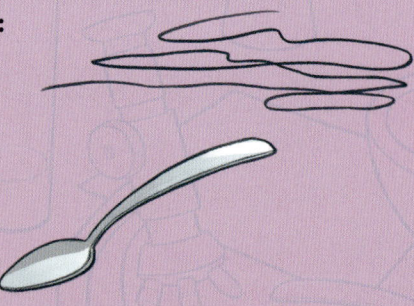

The Experiment

1. Tie the handle of the spoon to the middle of a piece of string.

2. Hold one end of the string against your left ear and the other end against your right ear. Gently swing the string so the bowl of the spoon hits the edge of a wooden table or chair. You should hear a sound like a bell.

Travelling toothpicks

Some substances interact with water in unusual ways. Soap dissolves in water and then spreads out over its surface.

You will need:
- Toothpicks
- Bowl of water
- Bar of soap

The Experiment

1. Float about eight toothpicks on the surface of the water.

2. Dip the soap in the middle of the water. The toothpicks will move out towards the sides of the bowl. This is because the soap is spreading out over the surface of the water and pushing the toothpicks apart as it goes.

Coin drop

Wooden objects, like toothpicks, consist of lots of tiny tube-like cells. Water can be sucked into the tubes by a process called 'capillary action'. This makes the wood swell and can make it move.

You will need:
- Toothpick
- Bottle
- Coin

The Experiment

1. Bend a wooden toothpick in half, being careful not to break it completely. Place the toothpick on top of a bottle.

2. Place a small coin on top of the toothpick. Now challenge your friends to come up with a way of making the coin fall into the bottle without touching any of the objects. Then show them how it is done.

3. All you have to do is pour some water onto the 'bend' in the toothpick.

4. As if by magic the tooth pick will move open and the coin will drop into the bottle.

Immoveable coin

Inertia is the property of a stationary object to remain stationary until it is forced to move. This tendency can be shown with simple household objects.

You will need:
- Card
- Large coin
- Scissors

The Experiment

1. Cut the card into a square measuring about 8cm x 8 cm. Balance the card on the tip of your left forefinger. Place the coin on the card directly above the tip of your finger. With the second finger of the right hand give the card a sharp flick.

2. The card will fly away but the coin will remain on the top of your finger because of inertia. Practice this to see how hard you have to flick the card to get the experiment to work.

Hole in the hand

If each eye is looking at something different, the brain merges the two pictures together to create a composite image. Sometimes this gives rise to strange optical illusions that show the brain at work.

You will need:
- Thin card
- Paperclips

The Experiment

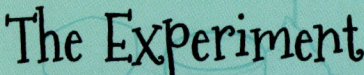

Roll the card into a tube. Use the paper clips to hold the tube shape together. Look through the tube with your left eye. Place your right hand against the tube with the palm towards your face.

Look through the tube and at your hand at the same time. It will seem that there is a hole in your right hand.

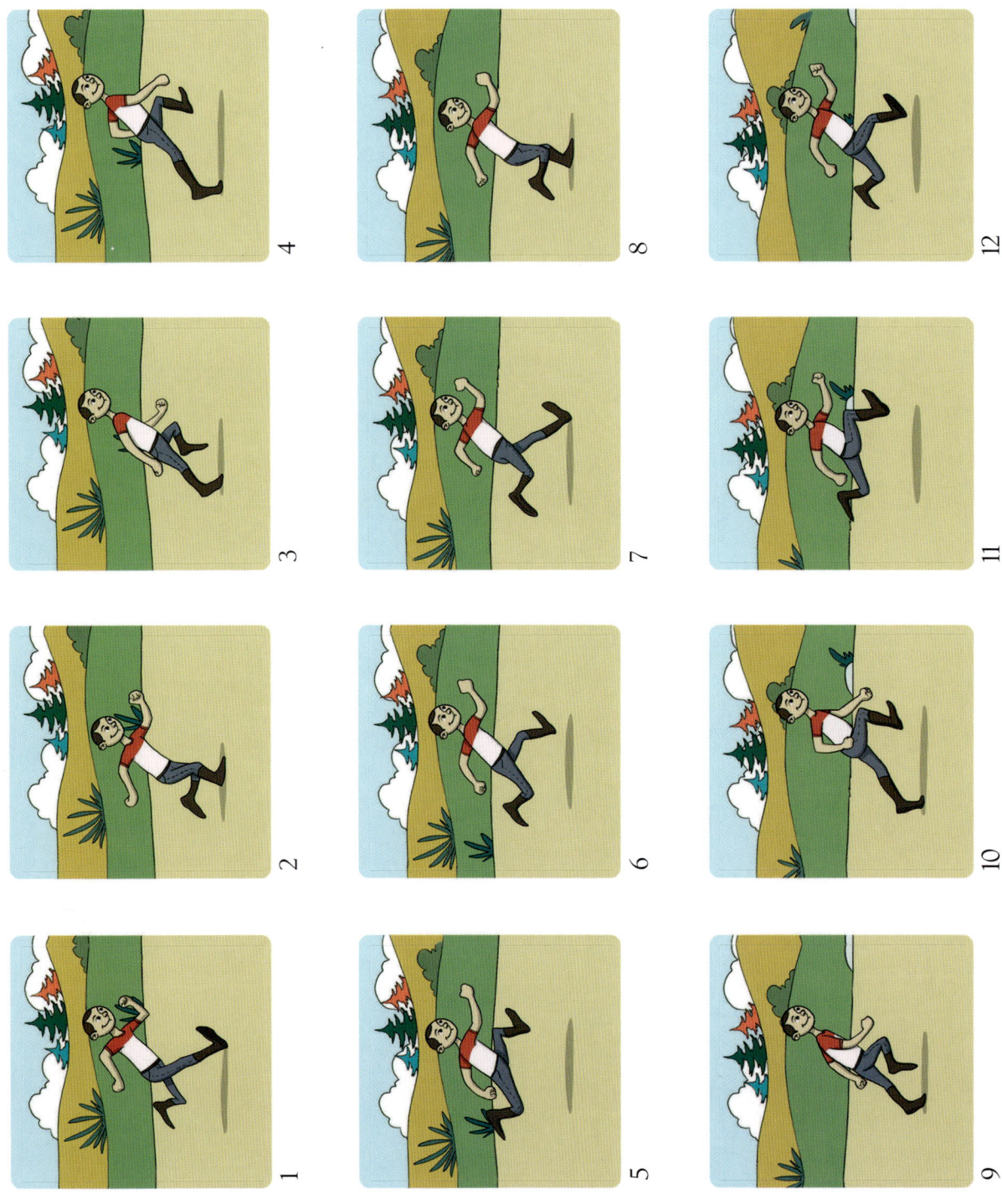

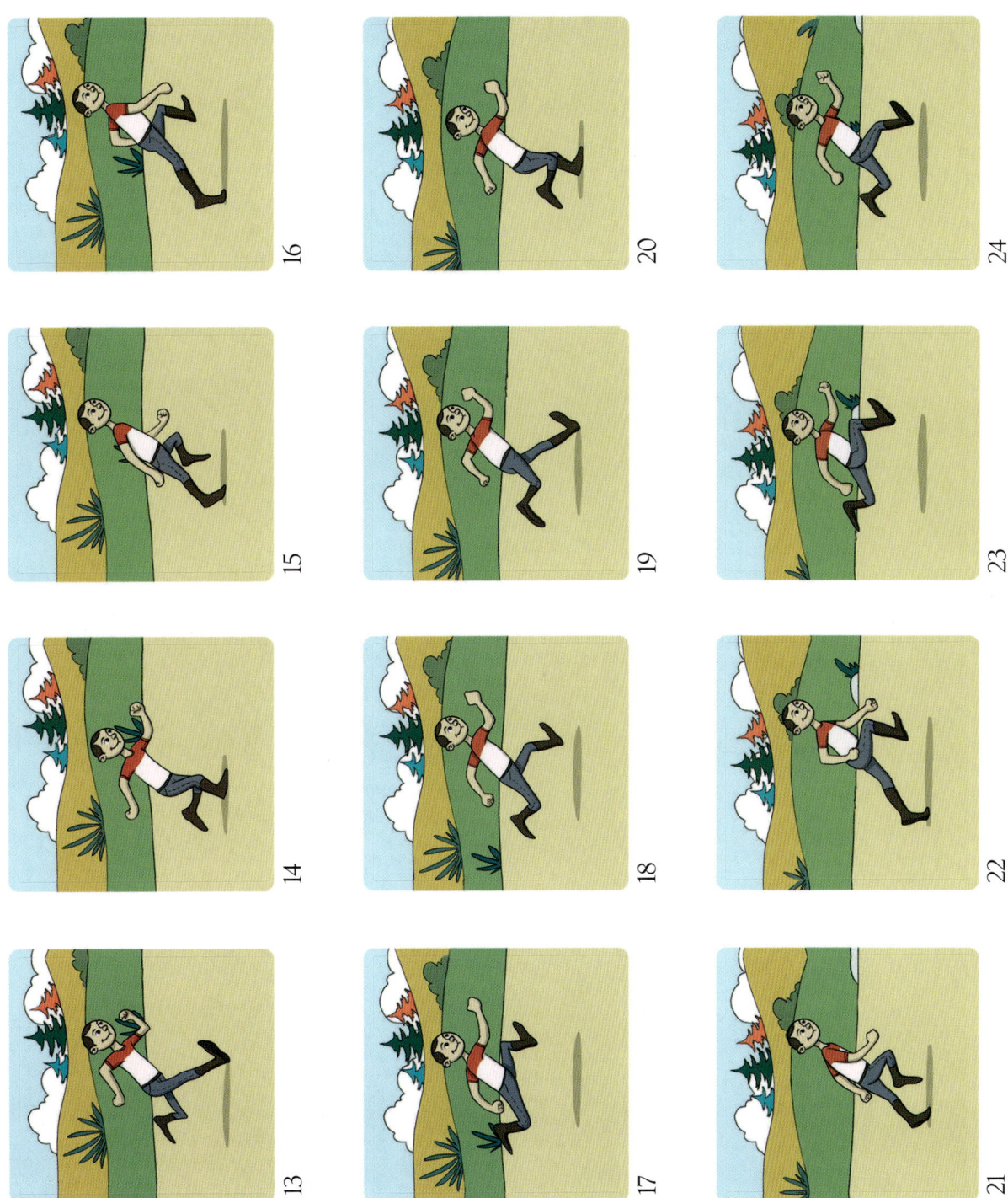

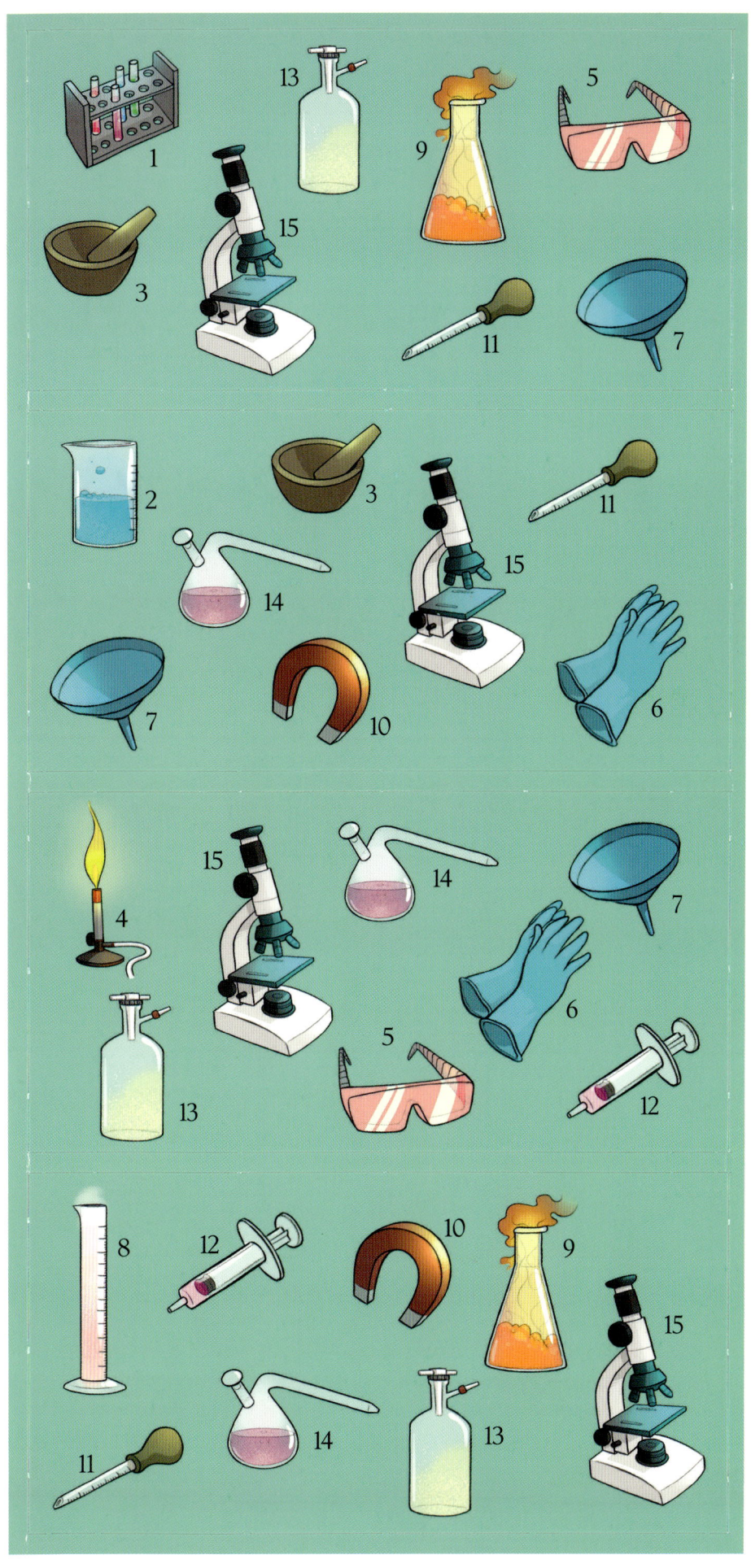

Instrumental

You will need:
- The templates on page 17
- Thin card
- Scissors
- A photocopier
- Some mental arithmetic

This is really just a good party trick. Impress your friends with your ability to tune into their brains!

The Experiment

1. Photocopy the 'instrument' pictures (p.17) onto thin card and cut it into four separate cards. Give the cards to a friend and ask him or her to choose one of the scientific instruments pictured on the cards without telling you which one.

2. Ask your friend to hand you all the cards that show their chosen instrument. All you have to do is mentally add up the numbers in the top left corner of each card. The total will give you the number of the instrument they have chosen.

3. If, for example, the cards you are given have the numbers 4 and 8 in the top left hand corners, you add them together to get 12. Number 12 is the syringe so you know this is your friend's chosen instrument.

Use your 'acting' skills to pretend you are sensing your friend's thought processes. **Never** mention any numbers!

Curious curves

You will need:
- Templates (p.19)
- Pencil
- Paint and paintbrush

This is a simple optical illusion or trick of the eye created by using two curved cards. Because the top curves are longer than the bottom ones, this tricks the brain into thinking that one of the cards is bigger than the other.

The Experiment

1. Push out the two curved templates on page 19. Paint one blue and one red (or any other colours you like).

2. Hold the red one above the blue one. The blue one will look longer than the red. Now hold the blue one above the red one. Now the red one looks the longer of the two!

Fish in a bowl

You will need:
- Thin card
- Scissors
- Pencil or crayon
- Thread or string

Although this optical illusion features two separate pictures, you see only one when the card is in motion. This is due to retention of vision. The card spins so fast that the brain cannot keep up and merges the two pictures together.

The Experiment

1. Cut a square piece of thin card about 5cm x 5 cm.

2. Make a small hole in each side of the card and thread string through the holes, making a loop on each side.

3. On one side of the card draw a large fish bowl and on the other side draw a small fish.

4. Wind up the two string loops as far as possible then let the card spin. You will be able to see the fish in its bowl now!

Make a flipbook

This is another example of retention of vision. The flipbook, like a cine film, is made up of lots of still pictures. When a film is screened or a flipbook is flicked, the images move fast enough to create the illusion of movement.

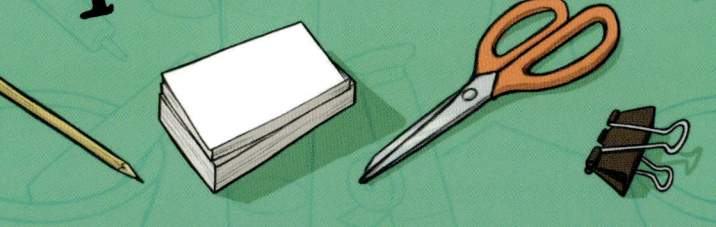

You will need:
- Thick paper or thin card
- Scissors
- Pen or pencil
- Bulldog clip

The Experiment

1. Cut the card or paper into 24 rectangles measuring 4cm x 8 cm. Now add the stickers from pages 14 and 15 to each one (in sequence).

2. Use the bulldog clip to hold all the images together.

3. Your flipbook begins with the last page. Use your thumb to flick quickly through the pages from back to front and the pictures will appear to move.

If you are good at drawing you can devise your own pictures of people, animals, cars and many other things to make your own flip books.

If you are not good at drawing keep your subjects simple - like a bouncing ball or just a squiggly line that changes.

Each drawing must be in the same position on the page but slightly different from the one before it.
If the movement is too slow or too jumpy, just add extra pages with very slight changes.

Egg-speriment

An object's density depends upon how solid it is. All things are made of molecules (small particles) and the more molecules there are the denser the object is. An object that is more dense than water will sink. But if the water is made denser than the object, then it will float.

You will need:
- Jar of water
- Egg
- Salt
- Spoon

The Experiment

1. Pour some water into a jar and then carefully place an egg in the liquid. It will drop to the bottom of the jar because the egg is denser than the water.

2. Remove the egg.

3. Now put two or three spoonfuls of salt into the water and give it a good stir.

26

It's a Fact

The Dead Sea in the Jordan Rift Valley is so salty that a person will automatically float in it. This is because the density of the water is greater than that of a human body so the body floats, just like the egg in this experiment. The Dead Sea is actually a lake and it gets its scary name because no plants or fish can live in it as it is so salty.

4

4. Put the egg back in the water and, amazingly, it no longer sinks — it actually floats!

Fantastic fish

You will need:
- Fish template
- Bowl of water
- Washing-up liquid (or oil)

In 1687 the British scientist Sir Isaac Newton said that for every action there is an equal and opposite reaction. This experiment shows this scientific principle at work.

The Experiment

1. Push out the fish template on page 30.

2. Lay the fish on top of the bowl of water, taking care not to get the top surface wet.

3. Carefully pour a small amount of washing-up liquid into the hole at the centre of the fish.

4. The washing-up liquid will try to spread out across the water. Its only way out of the centre is through the narrow slit towards the tail.

5. As the washing-up liquid pushes backwards, the fish begins to move forward in the opposite direction.

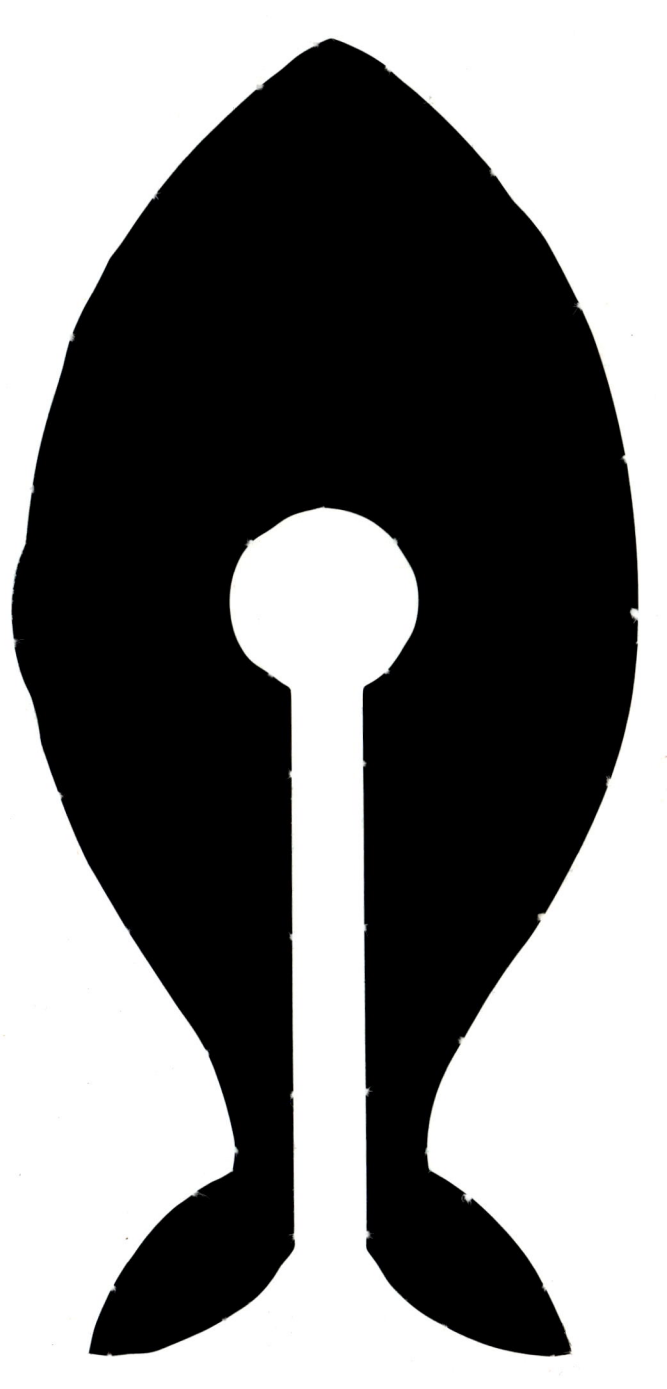

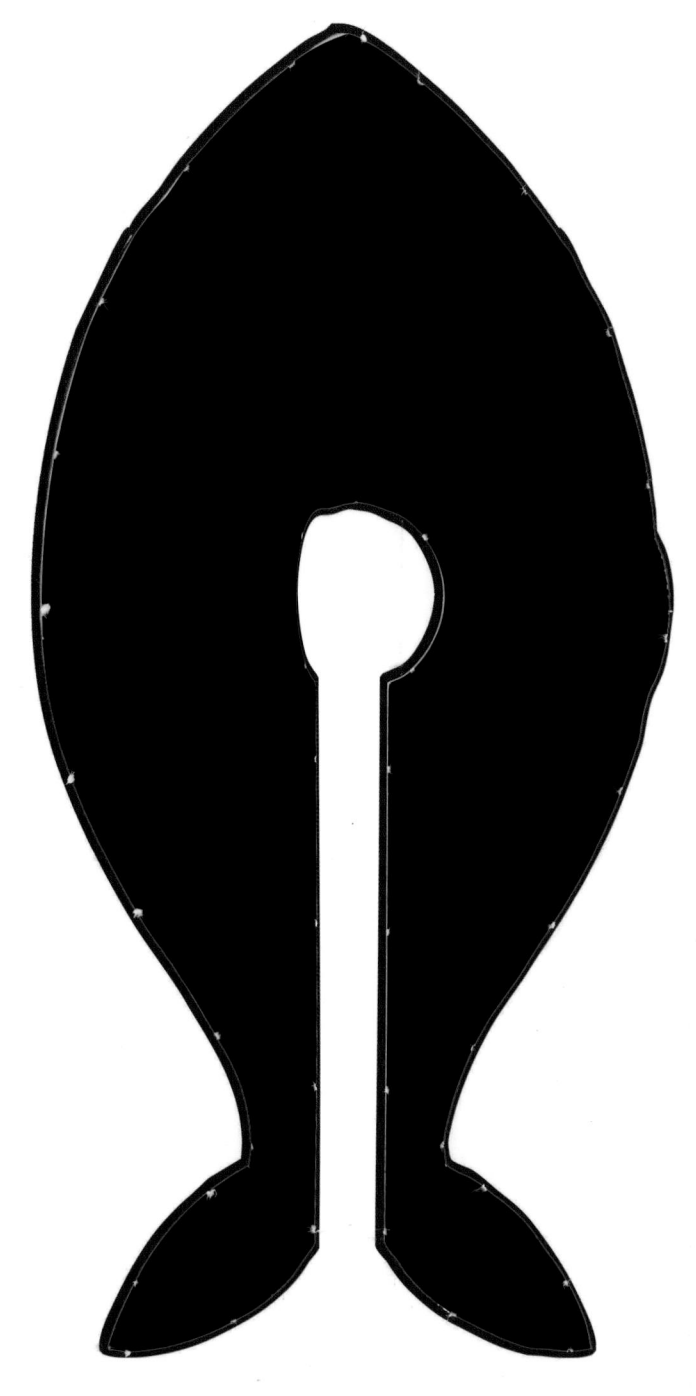

One good turn

You will need:

- Card
- Pen or pencil
- Glass tumbler
- Jug of water

Light waves travel in straight lines. But when light passes from the air into something else, such as water, it bends. This is called refraction. It can be shown very easily.

The Experiment

1. Draw a large arrow on a piece of card.

2. Hold the card behind the tumbler and check the direction of the arrow.

3. Now pour some water into the tumbler and the arrow will turn to point in the opposite direction.

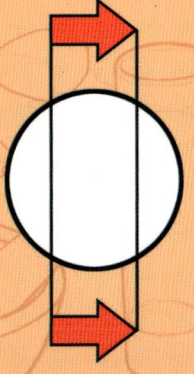

Under pressure

You will need:
- Two identical-sized sink plungers

This experiment with two sink plungers reveals the force of atmospheric pressure. This is the pressure created by the weight of air in the atmosphere. We don't notice it because we are used to it, but it is there all the same!

The Experiment

1. Wet the edges of both plungers and then press them together, mouth to mouth, as hard as you can.

2. Now try to pull them apart and you will find it very difficult, if not impossible. Even with someone else pulling on one of the plungers they are unlikely to budge.

It's a Fact

In 1654 the German scientist Otto von Geuricke gave a spectacular demonstration of the power of air pressure at Magdeburg, in Germany.

He used two hemispheres made of copper which he placed together.

Grease was used to create a good seal and then all the air was removed from the hemispheres.

Two teams of eight horses were used to try to pull the hemispheres apart but were unable to do so.

Defying gravity

The great British scientist Isaac Newton (1642 - 1727) was the first person to explain the force of gravity on objects. In this experiment, it is the force of gravity pulling the stone downwards (like all objects) that moves the box in a surprising direction!

You will need:
- A round cheese box
- A stone
- Modelling clay
- Sheet of thick card
- Block of wood (or a book)
- Pencil

The Experiment

1. Use some modelling clay to attach the stone to the inside of the box.

2. Put the lid on the box. Place a small pencil mark on the lid to show where the stone is positioned.

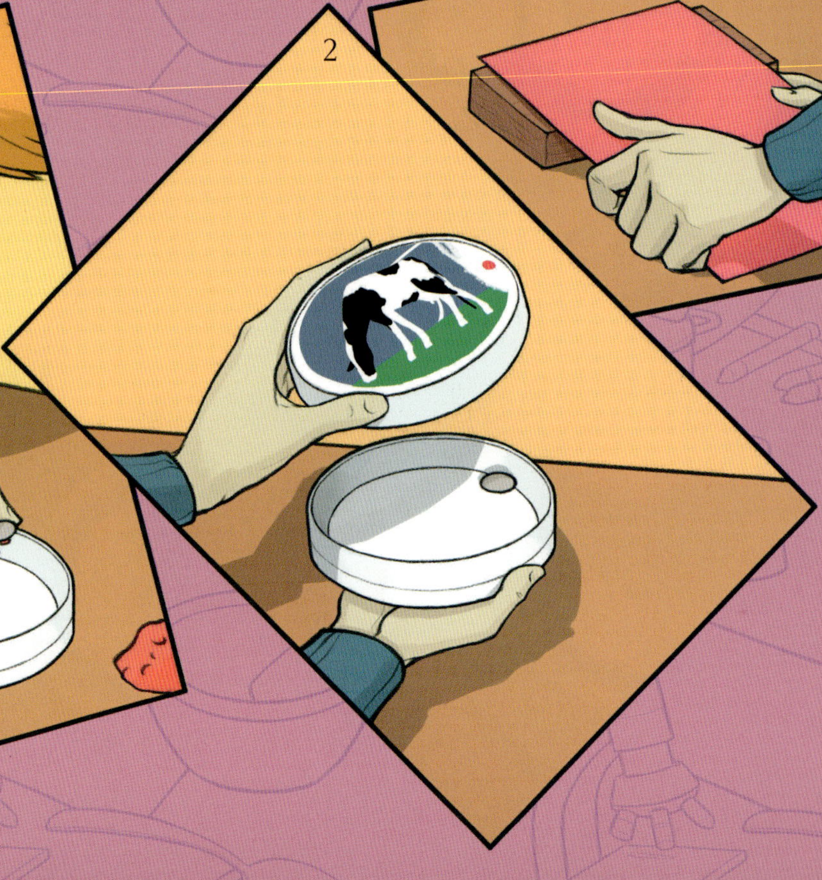

3. Lay one end of the card on the block of wood to make a sloping surface.

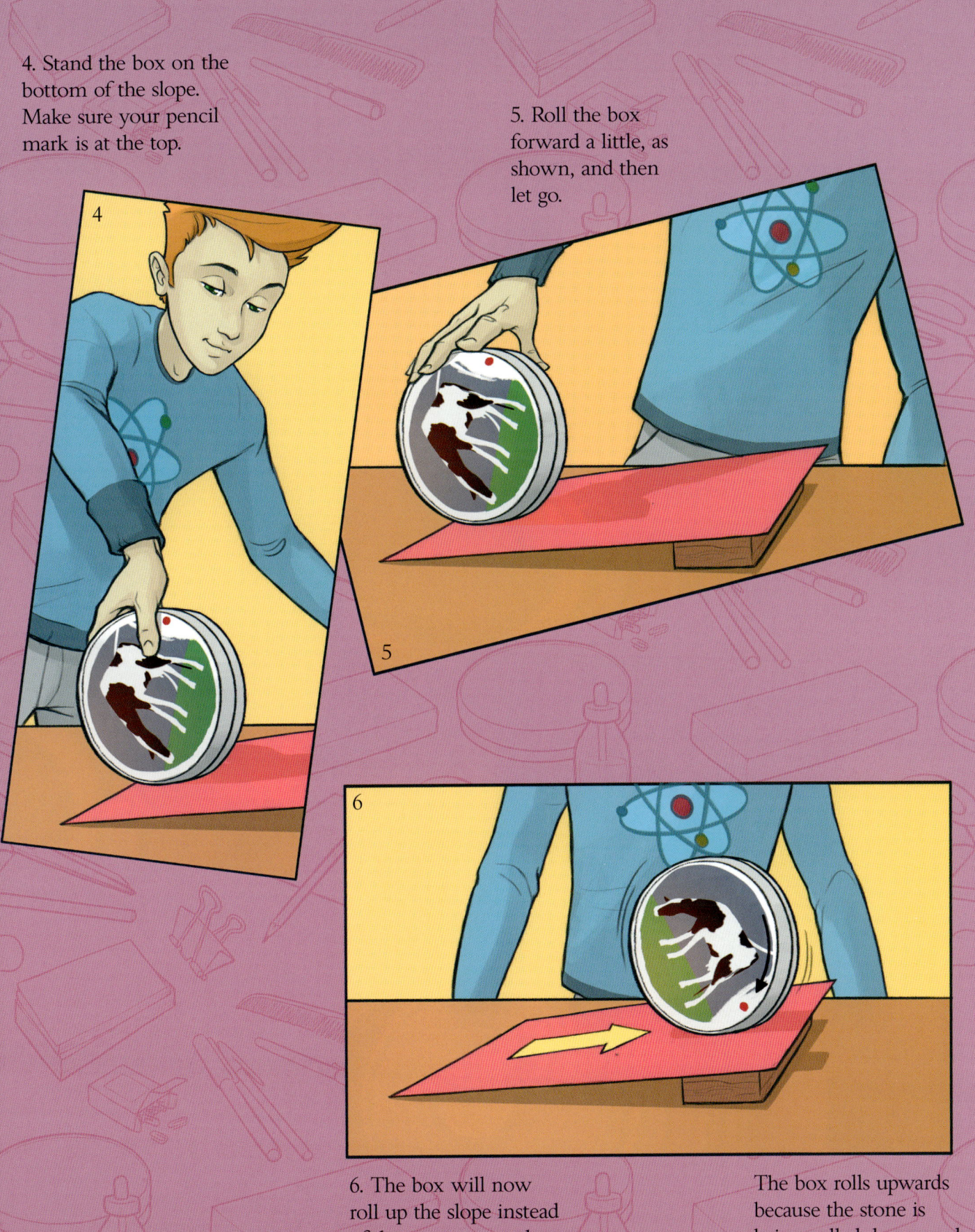

4. Stand the box on the bottom of the slope. Make sure your pencil mark is at the top.

5. Roll the box forward a little, as shown, and then let go.

6. The box will now roll up the slope instead of down as expected.

The box rolls upwards because the stone is being pulled downwards by the force of gravity.

Floating clip

You will need:
- Two paper clips
- Bowl of water
- Tissue paper
- Pencil

Although you can't see it, there is something like a thin skin on the surface of water. This is called 'surface tension' and it is strong enough to support small objects, as this experiment will show.

The Experiment

1. Take a small sheet of tissue paper and float it on the water.

2. Gently place a paper clip on the tissue.

3. Use the pencil to carefully push the tissue paper under the water. The paper clip will stay afloat!

It's a Fact

Surface tension is the reason why some insects are able to walk on water!

Straw of strength

E ven though we usually think of air as being light and insubstantial, it can exert amazing force and pressure when concentrated.

You will need:
- Plastic drinking straw
- Large potato
- A finger

The Experiment

Hold an unpeeled potato in one hand. Hold a plastic drinking straw in the other hand. Can you push the straw through the potato? The straw will just crumple up - unless you know this secret.

The straw must be held upright, but the real secret is that you hold your finger over the top end of the straw. This stops any air escaping and you can now drive the straw into the potato.

It takes some practice but you should soon get the knack, much to the amazement of your friends.

Ice up

You will need:
- Ice cube
- String
- Glass of water
- Salt

Salt water freezes at a lower temperature than non-salty water. Lakes, and even rivers, will freeze because they do not contain as much salt as the sea. As it contains a lot of salt, the sea seldom freezes. This experiment shows salt's effect on frozen water.

The Experiment

1. Put an ice cube in a glass of water.

2. Give someone the piece of string and challenge them to use it to lift the ice out of the water. They are not allowed to use a spoon, knife, fork or their fingers. When everyone has failed to do it, you show them how it can be done.

3. Pour some salt onto the ice cube and rest the string on top of it. The salt will melt the top surface of the ice cube.

4. Then, as the melted water dissolves the salt, it freezes over again and the string becomes stuck to the ice. This makes it possible to lift the cube from the glass.

Bending water

You will need:
- Plastic comb
- Water tap

An electrical charge can act like a magnet, attracting water towards it. This experiment lets you observe this strange effect.

The Experiment

1. Turn the tap on to produce a thin, steady flow of water.

2. Run the comb through your hair a few times to give it an electrical charge.

3. Hold the comb near, but not in, the stream of water. Watch the water bend towards the comb.

Flower power

You will need:

- A white carnation or other flower
- Red food colouring
- Two jars of water

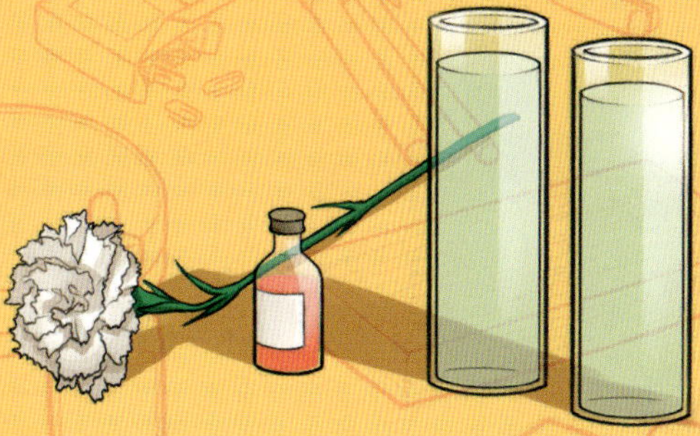

Water goes up a plant by a process called 'capillary action'. Inside the stem of a plant are narrow tubes. Because they are very narrow the water is forced upwards. These carry water to feed the plant. By using food colouring you can observe this process.

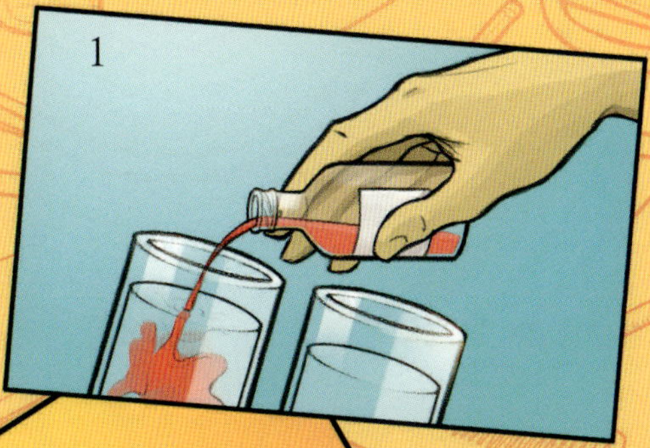

The Experiment

1. Put red food colouring in one of the jars of water.

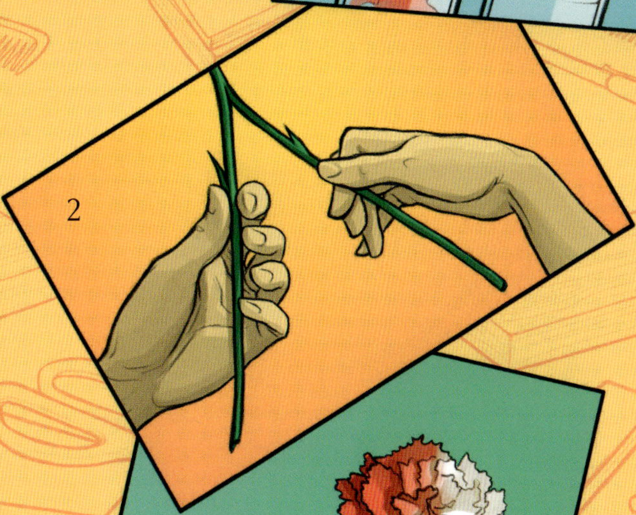

2. Carefully split the stem of the flower lengthwise.

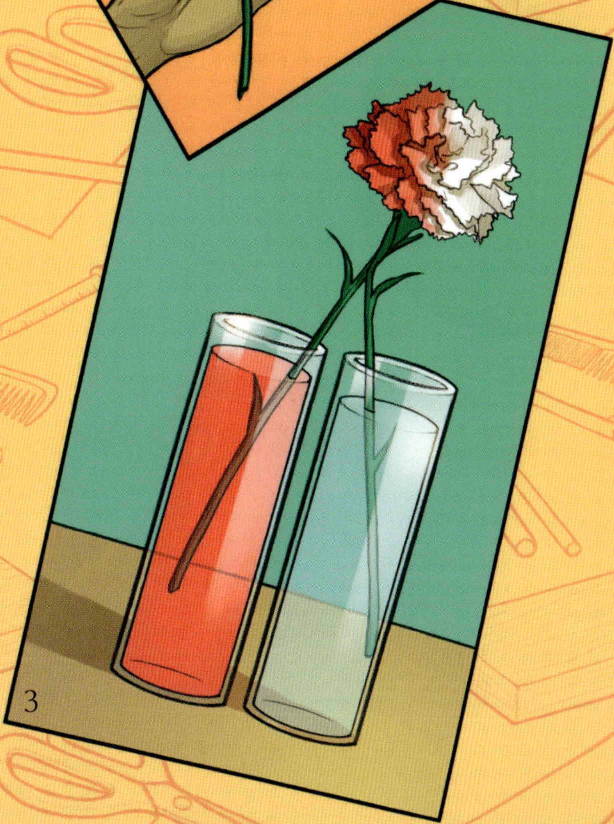

3. Put one half of the stem in one jar and the other half in the second jar. After a short while you will see that the half which is drawing up the coloured water is now red!

Flying sausage

You will need:
- Two hands
- Two eyes

The two separate images seen by each of your eyes can sometimes be made to combine in ways that create odd optical illusions.

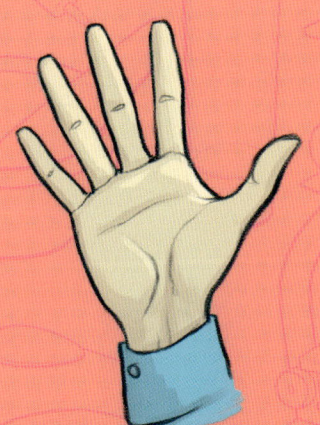

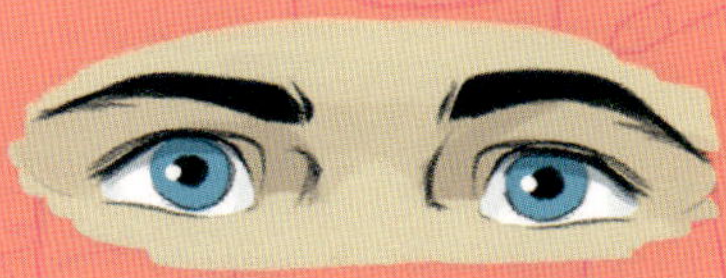

The Experiment

Hold your hands in front of your face. Extend both forefingers so they are touching. Look at something beyond your fingers. Now move your hands apart slightly. With a bit of luck you will see a small sausage shape floating between your fingertips.

Musical glass

Vibrations through objects often result in noises. This famous experiment shows how it is possible to even produce music from vibrations through simple household items.

The Experiment

Dip a forefinger in the water and rub it around the rim of the glass in a regular, continuous movement. With practice you will be able to produce a noise from the glass. Thin glasses and wine glasses produce the best sounds. Vary the amount of water in the glass to produce a different sound.

Making a zoetrope

T he zoetrope works in the same way as a flip book. Seeing the different images quickly gives the illusion of movement.

The Experiment

1. Make a hole in the centre of the base of the box. Stick a washer on the thin end of the chopstick until it will go no further. Push the thin end of the chopstick through the hole up to the washer.

You will need:
- Circular box
- Card template (p.32)
- Chopstick
- Metal washer
- Scissors
- Sticky tape
- Paper
- Pencil, paint or crayons

2. Press out the card template on page 32.

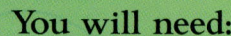

3. Roll up the card template so it will fit inside the box. Cut the paper into a strip that fits inside the black template, as shown.

It's a Fact

Zoetropes and other optical toys were very popular in the 19th century. There was no television then!

4. Remove the strip and draw pictures on it as you did for the flip book on pages 24 and 25. Each drawing should be the same distance apart as the slits in the black template.

5. Hold the chopstick in one hand and use your free hand to spin your zoetrope. Look through the slits and your pictures will seem to move. You can make other strips with different pictures on them.

Seeing is disbelieving

Do you believe everything you see? Well, you shouldn't.
Your brain sometimes plays tricks on you as these pictures
show. Photocopy them to show to your friends.

It looks as if the bottom horizontal
line is the longer of the two. Measure
them and you will find that they are
both the same length.

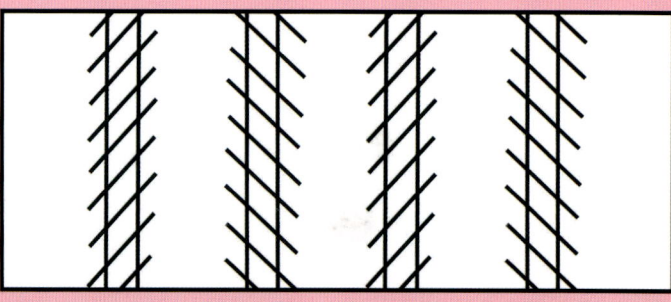

The long black lines are parallel, but they look as if
they are leaning different ways. Your brain is being
confused by the angle of the short lines. Check it
out with a ruler.

The centre dot on the right looks
larger than the centre one on
the left. Measure them - they are
both the same size!

Is this a rabbit facing left or a
duck looking to the right? Your
brain will not be able to make
up its mind!

Is the spine of this book
pointing towards you or away
from you? Your brain will keep
changing what it sees.

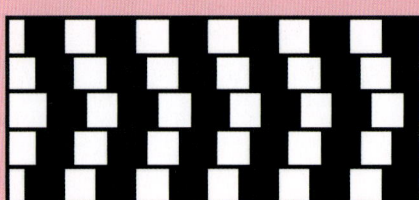

The horizontal lines of squares
look wider at one end than the
other. Check them with a ruler -
they are really parallel.

Can you see the white triangle? Look
closer - there is really nothing there.
Your brain has drawn it in for you!